J·O·Y

COMES

IN THE

MORNING

A BOOK FOR THOSE WAITING
FOR THE SUN TO RISE.

Love and Joy in Jesus,
Marjorie Meachum Fedor

MARJORIE MEACHUM FEDOR

J·O·Y
COMES
IN THE
MORNING

A BOOK FOR THOSE WAITING
FOR THE SUN TO RISE.

MARJORIE MEACHUM FEDOR

Joy Comes in the Morning
by Marjorie Meachum Fedor

Printed in the United States of America
ISBN 1-931232-38-5

Xulon Press
11350 Random Hills Road
Suite 800
Fairfax, VA 22030
(703) 279-6511
XulonPress.com

C·O·N·T·E·N·T·S

JOY COMES IN THE MORNING

God does not always protect us from heartaches,
but I can tell you first hand,

we grow,

we learn,

we change,

we have opportunities to become stronger and wiser.

When Paul says in 1 Thessalonians 5:18, "give thanks in
all circumstances," I understand this to mean that we
are to give thanks to God that He never leaves us. He is
surely with us in all things. I can promise you, God will
never fail you.

✳

"Weeping may remain for a night,
but rejoicing comes in the morning."
PSALM 30:5B

HOW IT ALL BEGAN....

As we all know, life brings a lot of ups and a lot of downs—bright days and dark nights.

Whether I find myself in the twilight of confusion and questioning, the early dawn of awe and hope, or the black midnight of fear and despair, I write...

It is like a letter to the Lord describing where I am. When I open my deepest self, Jesus meets me. He takes my spirit by the hand and leads me. And though my circumstances may at that moment appear unchanged, I begin to see new realities, my perception changes, and I change.

Over the years I have had occasions to share some of my writing with others. At their urging and after much prayer I have selected some of what I have written to share with you. It is a glimpse of God's grace in my life.

I hope you will find this little book to be a blessing.

In His love and service,

Marjorie Meachum Fedor

PROLOGUE

I hope that if God gives me enough time and spunk I will one day do something meaningful with the sundry things I have collected..

the pictures will go into albums,

the old embroidered handkerchiefs will be suitably displayed (or come back in style),

the sea shells and rocks will likely stay as they are (after all, they are meant to be picked up and tossed back at random).

But the collection of words that represent a part of me...that is harder.

Someday my children will go through all my collections and decide for themselves the value of each. I truly release them to do that. Treasure or trash it is for them to decide.

But the collection of words.. that is harder..they are windows into me.

Even so...

COMING FULL CIRCLE

I always knew I would grow older. I would get married and have children. I would go to school and work at some job or other...a nurse, a lawyer, a doctor, a decorator or maybe a secret agent. I would travel and do exciting things.

But, somehow, I thought that when I came back home it would be the same... my picture left no room for others to grow old, to change or to die. It left no room for buildings to be torn down, for roads to be widened, for interstates to be where the chickens roosted and the garden grew.

If I had understood that time was finite I might have appreciated more the old stories of " how it used to be," and I'm sure I would have learned the gardening secrets of my grandpa, in which phase of the moon to plant, and how deep, and when to harvest the potatoes and beans and turnips and that sweet, sweet corn. I would have learned the recipes for tea cakes, cherry winks and biscuits from grandma. I would have taken the time to

6

treasure the family and friends around me.

Now that life and age have brought me full circle, so much of what I knew is gone. I know better than to hope that others will learn from my story. Most will, themselves, have to come full circle to understand.

I'd like to find a lesson here though, to cushion this pesky feeling of regret. However, none comes to mind, so I'll take what I have and more fully appreciate it, and more fully value the parts of me made rich and strong by all that has gone on before, the good and the bad.

THE DISCOVERY

It was a sunny cool day, and the walk was invigorating her senses. As she made a turn, she stopped in her tracks in the middle of the gravel mountain road. She was caught by the sight of more butterflies than she had ever seen in one place, fluttering silently in and around a bright patch of yellow and white daisies. She wanted to leap gleefully into the middle of them, but she froze, fearful they would fly away and the moment would be lost.

It reminded her of times before when she felt so full of wonder that she thought she would surely burst if she did not express it. She was sure that whatever was waiting to be known was so magnificent that in comparison, fields of sunlit poppies would pale, and roaring waterfalls would whisper. She carried a delightful, powerful, inexpressible something deep within, secret even to her.

She had never found an avenue of expression. She

9

found instead a rather remarkable averageness, and had to remind herself often, in the face of great talent in others, of the "thou shalt not covet" commandment.

When she was young she had a great passion to play the piano. She practiced dutifully from the books recommended by Miss Minnie—the tall, straight, spinster lady with a bun at the nape of her neck, and with strong, thin fingers that precisely demonstrated the scales.

Nearly every Saturday morning for three years she had gone into town to meet Miss Minnie at the upright piano in her home across the park from Main Street. Ah, but it was not to be. The head, the heart and the hands never seemed to be in sync.

As a girl she was told she had a sweet voice. Perhaps that would be the answer. Singing might be the outlet she needed. She had a few lessons, sang in a wedding or two, a trio in high school, and various other places where sweet, young voices were appreciated. But alas, as she grew older, the melody that began at the diaphram as a strong, clear tone began to wobble as it made its way up and out. She carried a tune rather nicely, but no one would be inspired by the message. She was comforted to know she could at least contribute to the joyful noise offered to the Lord.

She tried dance. It was personally satisfying but certainly not stellar. Art was not even in the running. Sports? Not hardly. However, she did win a floating contest once in college. It turned out that she could float stiller and longer than any other contestant. It was something, but not likely to be a vehicle of expression. Besides, those jokes about being full of hot air promised to get old.

As time passed and life made its imprint, she continued her search for an outlet for that mysterious something that wants to be known. She had been to the Lord more times than she could count...cajoling, even chiding (she was ashamed to say). How, after all, was she to serve Him if she was given no talent, no tools, no anything of any consequence?

In time it became clear that God was saying, "I have given you your life! Come close to Me and I will shine through you. The mystery? You may not ever fully grasp it, but as you yield yourself to Me, others will glimpse it through you, and be drawn to Me. Your life is the instrument I will use to play a sweet song for others to hear, paint a picture for others to see, weave a fine, soft fabric for others to touch."

At first she felt great relief. All she had to do was offer her life and the Lord would use it. What could be easier than that? Then she looked at her life and was overwhelmed with sadness and shame when she saw the dark places in the corners that would surely block the light and make her useless.

Jesus looked at her, smiled at her, took her hands and said, "If you will just accept Me, I will wash away all the sooty remains of your mistakes. Walk with Me, love Me, learn from My living Word."

She began to feel again, so full of wonder that she thought she would surely burst. And the poppies paled and the waterfalls whispered as she became aware of the magnificent, powerful, mysterious, inexpressible presence of the Holy Spirit of God.

LIFE DANCE

I am dizzy and confused with the dance.

The kaleidoscope of bittersweet colors spins and whirls
rose red, clear yellow, emerald green, sky blue, black
and glistening white.
All are here, and more flowing 'round me enveloping
my soul.
A moving masterpiece.

The sounds of music, old and new
voices, harsh and kind
city sounds and country
full and friendly, lean and lonely
all are here and more, lifting me, moving me through
crescendo and silence.
A soaring symphony.

Am I a part of this, or does it turn and move for itself,
unaware of my presence?
I shout in a silent soul cry—"I am here!"
I want to stay and take strength from the billowing,

shimmering, unbridled energy.
I am drawn into a knowing that God is in control of this
paradox of harmony and confusion, and my consuming
need to pull the strings, to fight the flow, to run the
show is given up.

I sense I am a part of the beauty, and the balance and
the brilliance
I am a part of the plan
I want to rejoice, but I hesitate...

I hear a voice... a clear voice of pure love...a strong yet
gentle voice "Welcome, will you come and dance with
me?"

Warm smiling eyes reassure me—strong arms embrace
me. I am swept securely into the dazzling brilliance of
the King's grand ballroom.

And I know..I know this is Jesus, the Prince of Peace, the
Christ, the Lord and my partner for the dance of life.

— Marjorie Meachum Fedor —

MORNING SONG

I sing my song in the
yellow-gray mist of
the morning.

I am lost…
Does anyone hear me?

✳

*"He put a new song in my mouth,
a hymn of praise to our God."*
PSALM 40:3

SUNRISE COLORS

The morning is soft with whispered promises of
strength and peace.

The fragile sunrise colors run and hide,
but the breath of God remains.

And I feel strong, and sure,
and filled with a love I do not understand.

✳

*"And the peace which transcends all understanding, will
guard your hearts and minds in Jesus Christ."*
PHILIPPIANS 4:7

THE SAFETY LINE

Imagine if you can the experience of being a circus performer, while having a safety line attached to you.

Now imagine further that you are experiencing life in all its fullest—every fierce storm and every gentle cool breeze, every dark cloud and every bright rainbow. You feel it all. You are in the middle of it all. You stumble and you soar.

But all the time you have a safety line made up of the Lord's promises and the Holy Spirit. It attaches with the double lock of your faith and God's unconditional love.

When we offer ourselves to Him, He claims us for His own, and nothing can separate us from His love and caring. It does not remove life's problems, but it does fill us with a peace that cannot be described—a solid quiet confidence in the midst of confusion. And we are power-filled and peace-filled.

"For I am convinced that neither death nor life, neither angels nor demons, neither the present nor the future nor any powers, neither height nor depth, nor anything else in all creation, will be able to separate us from the love of God that is in Christ Jesus our Lord."
ROMANS 8:38,39

THE WORRY WALL

I know my trouble is nothing compared to yours, if you're measuring how big troubles are. But this trouble is mine, and until I can find a way to resolve it, I am filled up with it. So filled, that even though I can see, and hear, and even touch you, I cannot really feel what you are feeling.

There is something very wrong about this. When I am unable to communicate and share, I am building a wall around myself. So what began as a "trouble" might soon become self-pity and lonely isolation.

But troubles come to us all. They are real. They are facts of life. To try and deny them is dishonest and unhealthy.

Then what is the answer?

Maybe it isn't the "trouble" that is causing the real problem, but my attitude toward it—my worry.

To worry is surely to lack faith. If my faith is intact, my

attitude toward problems is one of optimism and confidence. The Lord tells us to not worry, but to give our troubles to Him.

I don't know exactly how that works, but even as I sit here thinking about it, I can feel that it does. The wall comes down—the burden is lifted—thanks be to God.

❈

"Do not be anxious about anything, but in everything, by prayer and petition, with thanksgiving, present your requests to God."
PHILIPPIANS 4:6

❈

"In this world you will have trouble. But take heart! I have overcome the world."
JOHN 16:33B

FALLING APART

All around me my world is falling apart...it has anger and misunderstanding burning away at the center...vindictiveness and selfishness spewing forth such heat I can hardly breathe.

I want to be loving and gentle and strong...I want to be able to help those I love so dearly. But I have no control of it, and everything is crumbling around me.

How many times must I shake and cower in fear and helplessness?

Lord, hold on to me...hold my world together...help us so we do not cause pain for each other.

Be in control. Thank You, Jesus, for being here.

"For I am the Lord your God, who takes
hold of your right hand and says to you,
Do not fear; I will help you."
ISAIAH 41: 13

— Marjorie Meachum Fedor —

SHOW ME, LORD

Is a door closing?
Am I to turn in a new direction?
Show me, Lord. Help me, Lord!

He answers, "Wait on Me,
I will cause it all to happen.
It is for you to listen and follow."

✳

*"I will instruct you and teach you in the
way you should go; I will counsel you
and watch over you."*
PSALM 32:8

FAITH

I saw You there for a moment on the shore, I heard You beckon, "Come,"
and in a kind of carefree, happy faith, I stepped out.

The water was far from calm, and I was surely not dressed for swimming, but I had seen
Your face, and I had heard Your voice, so in a kind of buoyant faith, I swam on.

I keep getting more and more to carry. What do You want me to bring, what should I let go of?

That faceless darkness knows me well, and in its presence
I cannot tell Your will from mine.

I am drowning, God!!! I am struggling to find You. I want to give all this to You, but it is dark, and the water is so cold, and I am so very tired. I gasp for breath and meet the waves. I ache and burn inside. I want no more of this empty, lonely struggle. It is too much.

A glimmer of light. A tiny shaft of grace beams through and holds me fast. I know You are there. I know You are here. You have reached for me. I know for this moment I am safe.
That is all my faith can tell, but in this moment, it is enough.

I cried to the Lord and He answered. With the light of His love, He came down.
In the dark and the storm He is constant. By His grace I am safe evermore.

❋

"Though the mountains be shaken and the hills be remove, yet My unfailing love for you will not be shaken nor my covenant of peace be removed, "
says the Lord who has compassion on you."
ISAIAH 54:10

IN GOD'S HANDS

This pain is so enormous I cannot look at it.
I want it all to go away, but the siren brings it back
and tells me it is real.

My son may die. Or he may live, but not really be alive.

God, I don't know what to ask.

You love him even more than I do.
I place him in Your hands.
Let nothing happen that is not Your will.

Strengthen us that we may be able to accept Your will.

Give us the faith to know You are present
and that
You are now guiding all that is happening.

Please hold on to me…

"For I am the Lord your God, who takes hold
of your right hand and says to you,
Do not fear; I will help you."
Isaiah 41:13

✷

"When you pass through the waters,
I will be with you;
and when you pass through the rivers
they will not sweep over you."
Isaiah 43:2a

GOD'S GRACE

You have entered our lives, Lord, and the miracle has happened. "Awe" is probably the word to describe how I feel. I have never been this close to a real miracle before. I can see and touch where You have moved.

What do I do now? What did I do right to make this happen? What if I do something wrong and You take it away? What shall I do to pay for it? When will "the other shoe drop?"

I have known tragedy, and it was easier to understand than this. Somehow tragedy fits in this world of debts and payments.

I am unworthy…I have not earned this…I cannot pay for it.

But I am not supposed to pay, am I?

It is a gift, with nothing expected in return.

32

— Marjorie Meachum Fedor —

It is a gift of love.

It is God's grace.

✳

> *"For it is by grace you have been saved,*
> *through faith—and this not from yourselves,*
> *it is the gift of God."*
> EPHESIANS 2:8

GRADUATION

It is time…

The years have passed so quickly, and there are so many things I wish I had done and some I wish I had not done.

The question haunts me…have I helped you gain the right knowledge and learn the right skills…are you strong enough?

Would you listen to how pompous I sound!
As though I were programming a computer in a robot.

What I must realize is that from the time God gave you life He has been in charge of the direction. I thank Him for letting me be a part of it.

I will not presume to take the credit, nor to feel the guilt…I have done my parenting with love and faith, in the best way I knew. And I have come to realize that even though I can fail and you can fail, God never can.

We continue to travel on, but we must follow different paths. Your experiences and your goals will be your own...your faith in God and in yourself will grow as you personally experience life, and love, and God's constancy.

Though the world is the same, you may see it differently from where you stand. See how right that is...now with faith and respect and sharing, there can be added a new dimension to Frost's "roads in the yellow wood"...though each of us travels but one road, there can now be an understanding of another.

God is with you...if you listen you can feel the whisper of His voice.

"For I know the plans I have for you, declares the Lord, plans to prosper you and not to harm you, plans to give you hope and a future. Then you will call upon me and come and pray to me, and I will listen to you. You will seek me and find me when you seek me with all your heart."
JEREMIAH 29:11-13

— *Marjorie Meachum Fedor* —

I FIND MYSELF PRAYING

Sometimes I find myself praying
for those in the darkened house,
that they might find the switch and
turn on the brilliant light of Your love.

Then I look at myself in a gloriously lit room
with my eyes closed;
and I know who has further to go,
and the most to learn, and the greater need for prayer.

HIGH SEAS

I have lost my bearings
I can no longer see the shore
the seas are high and I am
weary of the struggle.

I am going to lie down now.
If there is a port You want me to reach,
You will have to get me there,
because I'm too tired.

If there is a dream You want me to dream
You must give it to me,
for I am exhausted from chasing
vague, illusive promises.

I breathe the air of this quiet, strangely,
lovely moment,
and I know it is all that I have ever been…
it is all that I have…it is all that I am.

*"He got up and rebuked the wind and the raging waters;
the storm subsided, and all was calm."*

LUKE 8: 24B

COURAGE

Courage begins when we can admit that there is no life without some pain, some frustration; that there is no tragic accident to which we are immune; and that beyond the normal exercise of prudence we can do very little, or nothing, about it.

But real courage goes beyond and sees that the triumph of life is not in pain avoided, but in joys lived completely in the moment of their happening.

Courage lies in never taking so much as a good meal, or a day of health and fair weather, for granted. It lies in learning to be aware of our moments of happiness as sharply as our moments of pain. We need not be afraid to weep when we have cause to weep, so long as we can rejoice at every cause for rejoicing.

But how can I do this? I feel so inadequate and frustrated at times....
I believe the answer is to allow God to be in control.

I believe the hollow, empty spaces inside us that cause weakness, are suppose to be filled with the Holy Spirit. When this happens it is the difference between sand and rock; between fear and courage. When the Lord said to Peter, "You are the rock," I think that is what He meant.

The Holy Spirit fills the spaces in the shifting sands of our souls and brings to us structure, solidity and strength.

✻

"Be of good courage, and He shall strengthen your heart, all ye that hope in the Lord."
PSALM 31:24 (NKJV)

✻

"Likewise, the Spirit also helps us in our weaknesses."
ROMANS 8:26

REUNION

The impressions of the last few days sit in a heap on the floor of my heart. My mind keeps trying to sort through them and my emotions keep them stirred.

Fewer were the men at the reunion this year and fewer wives of these heroes of WW II. These are the men of the 509th parachute battalion. They met in war to bring us peace and to preserve our freedom.

If they came together now for the first time they would likely have very little in common. But this is not the first time—they share a bond forged from life and death moments, uncommon courage, youthful bravado. They laugh at the stories they have all heard before, and know by heart and never tire of telling or hearing. There are many other stories that are unspoken even now. They silently and bravely carry the memories of the pain, the dirt, the blood, the fear, the fatigue, the sounds of battle, the times of eerie quiet. When they look each other in the face and grasp a hand and lift a glass those memories too are shared. These are the men whose wives and children and now grandchildren all say, "He never really talks about it very much. I sometimes hear about what he did from his old friends."

On one day of the reunion there was a mass parachute jump to honor these brave pioneers of the silk and the static line. Facing us, the honor guard stood silent and still in a grassy area a few hundred yards away. The planes circled once and when they came by again streams of troopers filled the sky. The white chutes of the '40's were replaced by the green camouflage of today. They landed out of sight over a ridge in the low rolling hills. Then we waited for the first sign of someone to come over the horizon. The old soldiers and their families waited alongside of the families of the young soldiers who had jumped. The color guard waited as their flags blew in the breeze. In the distance we saw them coming. A few at first and then as groups they assembled in full battle gear to their designated places. Those who were from the 509th rallied behind the color guard and finally they all marched forward toward the bleachers…. toward the honored men who had given so much nearly 60 years ago to pave the way for these young soldiers. We stood and applauded the old men, the young men and the moment.

There was a strange sense of past and present changing places, for hidden in the valiant heart and soul of each

old soldier is a tall, straight, strong, clear-eyed,
exuberant young man still bound by duty and honor
and love for his family, his friends and his country.

Thank you for your unselfish acts, your indomitable
spirit and the example you have set before us. May God
grant us the wisdom to learn from you.

For my dad, J. C. "Jim" Meachum,
Your loving daughter, Marjorie

GRIEF

Whether loss in our lives is announced and expected, or a sudden "bolt from the blue", the effect is essentially the same...we experience GRIEF. Grief is that painful, scary, confusing feeling of being disconnected and out of "sync" with ourselves and the world around us. In grief our basic need for belonging and balance becomes threatened.

This emotional balance may be upset by all sorts of losses: death, illness of family or friends, divorce, failing health, loss of job, relocation or any change from the familiar. The more intense the feeling of connectedness has been in the past, the deeper the feelings of loss. We can feel as though we are truly losing a part of ourselves.

All of us like to feel safe and in control of our lives and when life changing circumstances shake our security we are challenged to change, to grow, to trust, to be vulnerable, to strengthen our faith and often to let go of everything except God.

Even though each of us is unique, there are feelings and stages of grief that we may have in common with others as we walk that difficult road.

Often accompanying grief there is...

CONFUSION: this is characterized by disbelief, conflicting feelings and difficulty in focusing.

DENIAL: this serves the useful but temporary purpose of "softening the blow" and allows time to gather strength and other resources. The difficulty comes when we stay in denial too long..this may cause withdrawal, postponement of feelings, isolation and often blocks our path to healing.

FEAR: of the unknown, abandonment, loneliness, disconnected feelings, being out of control, pain (both physical and/or emotional).

GUILT: we may feel guilty because we remember past mistakes (real and imagined); we may judge ourselves as unworthy because we recognize our anger and "flimsy" faith; we may have unrealistic expectations of ourselves in that we have not been able to "make everything all right".

ANGER: this comes from fear and the sense of powerlessness. We ask "why?"...we are tempted to blame everyone and everything—even God. Anger is a normal emotion. When we honestly acknowledge and express it we prevent the harm that comes from denying or misdirecting it.

DEPRESSION: this is usually a result of denied and buried feelings and of prolonged feelings of helplessness. It is usually unfocused and we cannot seem to identify the source or find the way to fix it.

SADNESS: this differs from depression in that it is focused, and at times mixed with feelings of loneliness, or anticipated loneliness. It is often associated with memories and feelings of regret.

We may cycle through these stages more than once and sometimes in our attempt to avoid the hurt we may get lost and stuck. Grief is natural and normal, but even when we move through it in a healthy way the process brings stress. Stress is that place where the challenges of life meet our "store of resources". Stress is very real and can effect us physically, mental, emotionally and spiritually.

Here are some practical and helpful suggestions for building the store of resources when dealing with grief:

I. CALL ON GOD

He made us and understands this process better than
we do. His Word provides the foundation for our faith,
the strength for our growth, the courage to persevere,
and comfort in our sorrows. Jesus is the "keel" that
offers balance in the stormy sea.

"The Lord heals the broken hearted"
PSALMS 147:3

✳

*"When anxiety was great within me,
your consolation brought joy to my soul"*
PSALMS 94:19

✳

"I will never leave you or forsake you"
JOSHUA 1:5B

II. PRAY

*"I sought the Lord, and He answered me:
He delivered me from all my fears"*
PSALMS 34:4

III. MAKE AMENDS IF NEEDED

*"Bear with each other and forgive whatever
you have against each other"*
COLOSSIANS 3:13

IV. CRY…WALK…RELAX/BREATH…REST…
SLEEP…EAT SENSIBLY

Don't push yourself either physically or
emotionally…give yourself time.
Find opportunities to share laughter with others. A
smile is like a light in the dark of night.

*"A cheerful heart does good like a medicine,
but a broken spirit makes one sick."*
PROVERBS 17:22

V. GET EXTERNAL SUPPORT THROUGH HONEST
SHARING WITH FRIENDS, FAMILY, CLERGY,
SUPPORT GROUPS OR A PROFESSIONAL
THERAPIST

VI. LOOK AT THE BIG PICTURE AND KNOW THAT
GOD IS FAITHFUL

Often, in our fear of aloneness and of loneliness, we fill every moment with activities and human relationships. Schedules become so full there is no room for God's plan to be worked out in our lives.

Never think He has deserted you because He has a plan for you with every detail worked out. It is possible to become so encumbered by our self-prescribed "treatments" that we miss God's best for our lives.

Do not rush to healing. Instead rush to God because that is where you will find the healing.

So wait until the *darkness of mourning* changes to become the *light of the morning*.

"Though the mountains be shaken and the hills be removed, yet my unfailing love for you will not be shaken nor my covenant of peace be removed, says the Lord who has compassion on you."
Isaiah 54:10

✳

"Trust in the Lord with all your heart and lean not on your own understanding.
Proverbs 3:5

Remember, grief is not a "black hole"….. it is more like a passageway…dark and scary perhaps, but we can move through it to healing, peace, joy and wholeness.

FAITH IN SADNESS

There is a sadness I cannot describe
when I see how wrong some things are.

And a sadness even greater when I
know not how I might have changed it.

May God and my family
forgive me my mistakes.

God, please lift me from this valley
to a soaring faith—a faith that You
will transform the mistakes I have made into blessings.

Thank You, Lord.

"Whenever our hearts condemn us,
God is greater than our hearts and
He knows everything."
1 JOHN 3:20

✻

"The Lord is close to the brokenhearted
and saves those who are crushed in spirit."
PSALM 34:18

ALONE WITH THE LORD

Lord, I know You are with me, but I still feel alone. I know that I shouldn't, but I still feel alone. I have been alone so much it seems, with You my only strength, and when I shut You out I am without strength or comfort.

I know You are with me now and I am thankful. But how I long to share, really share my life, my burdens and joys with another person. I wonder if maybe You have been showing me for a long time that we all travel this life "alone." We have parents, we have friends, we marry and have children, we have strong ties to one another, and our love and caring are great—but we are still "alone."

Have You been showing me that Your Presence is the only truly constant companion we have, or need?

I think You are saying to me, "If you are filled with My Spirit, and My peace, there can be no loneliness, even when it seems to you, that you are alone. And the love you have for those around you will be complete through Me."

Thank You Lord. Help me, Lord.

✳

"Peace I leave with you; my peace I give to you.
I do not give to you as the world gives.
Do not let your hearts be troubled
and do not be afraid."
JOHN 14:27

✳

"I will never leave you nor forsake you."
HEBREWS 13:5B

GOD'S PEACE

The window shades of doubt—
Each one I pull dims,
then finally blackens, my room—my very soul.

God's Peace—
The warm, golden, radiant light
that embraces my soul and fills my room.

✹

*"In Him our hearts rejoice for
we trust in his holy name."*
PSALM 33:21

DARKNESS IN THE NIGHT

What darkness is this that hides in the night unseen, what hands are these that reach, then lift me down, that caress and delude?

What wine is this that lulls my mind and hungers for itself?

This cushioned ride to empty lonely torment keeps its secret well to see the darkness only when the morning fails to come.

Faith wars with anguish on this road through chaos and despair.

But the Light circles down and around and gently lifts, growing stronger and brighter, healing the pain, erasing fearsome shadows.

The sun is bright and warm now. It colors my world.

My heart smiles with love and peace.

Night will come again, and with it may come darkness,
but a soul once touched, glows with an awesome,
stubborn light that changes darkness into silver white.

❋

"You, O Lord, keep my lamp burning;
my God turns my darkness into light."
PSALM 18:28

❋

"God…has called you out of darkness
Into his wonderful light."
1 PETER 2: 9B

JOYFUL PEACE

I feel so at peace
yet filled with
a joyful unrest

So like the ocean, where
there is such power
and such serenity

I cannot of myself feel
this calm in the midst
of crisis and confusion

Truly there is a resource
beyond my understanding,
There is God, and He is here.

✳

"Surely then you will find delight in the Almighty
and you will lift up your face to God."
JOB 22: 26

LIVING IN THE LIGHT

Like warm sunshine, you touched a dormant
seed, and I have grown..
I would like to think I did something of the
same for you.

But, for any plant to flourish and bloom it
must have roots.
It must be nurtured by light and gentle rain.
It cannot survive in the shadows.

We too must have light or our spirits will
surely fade and die.

Though the wall between us is not high,
     nor the gate locked, it must stay closed.
For now we have colorful, fragrant gardens
     of our own to tend.
For now there is the touch of lovely memories
     across the fence.
And that is enough.

"Come...let us walk in the light of the Lord."
ISAIAH 2:5

✴

"Blessed is the man who perseveres under trial,
because when he has stood the test, he
will receive the crown of life that God has
promised to those who love Him."
JAMES 1:12

ALONE AGAIN

Alone with this desperate emptiness
even to cry alone.

Why did You bring wholeness back into focus,
into color,
yet keep it just beyond my touch...
"See, this is what is possible,
but not for you! Never for you!"

Again I'll cry awhile, and then I'll smile
 (I'm good at that),
I'll "fluff my feathers" (I've had life-long practice),
and no one will know that just under the surface
it is all a tragic comedy...
for me to teach the beauty of being
while I grow so weary of being.

For me where is the light,
where is the completeness?
Is it an illusive obvious, or is it for me a mirage?
When I get there it is gone,

a mere reflection of someone else's reality.

Oh, God,
please hear me
please help me…

※

"The Lord is a refuge for the oppressed,
a stronghold in times of trouble.
Those who know your name will trust in you,
for you, Lord, have never forsaken
those who seek you."
PSALM 9:9,10

— Marjorie Meachum Fedor —

THE TANGLED BALL
OF YARN

It is so frustrating to stand
here in the middle of this mess
and not know how to unravel it.

It is like a big tangled ball of yarn
with many different pieces.
If I pull on one piece I tighten another;
Loosen one and another gets in a knot.

The only way to straighten it out, it seems,
Is to relax the hold I have on it.

✳

*"Cast your cares on the Lord and He
will sustain you."*
PSALM 55: 22

HOLES IN MY BEING

I struggle against the wind and I am tired.

My shelters, my hiding places,
appear to be full already, or out of reach.

Ugly

Jagged

Gaping

HOLES IN MY BEING

So many painful losses
deceptively covered over by
the pretty tissue paper of stoic,
smiling, civility,
most times fooling even me.

*"My flesh and my heart may fail,
but God is the strength of my heart and
my portion forever."*
PSALM 73: 26

— *Marjorie Meachum Fedor* —

MORNING MIST

This wistful sadness is like a gentle
morning mist,
it softens all the lines, and sounds and colors,
and there is but a bit of glow to mark
the sun's place.

Like all morning mists, this one too shall rise,
leaving me immersed in sparkling,
brilliant hues,
with a view of the road that is crystal clear.

But for now, there is the quiet,
and the cool stillness of this moment.

"And the peace of God,
which passeth all understanding,
shall keep your hearts and minds
through Christ Jesus."
PHILIPPIANS 4: 7

WHITE WATER

Floating on the crest of rapid white water,
hitting rocks, spinning 'round,
hanging on, so afraid.

It's so hard to remember,
so hard to imagine
peace and calm and joy.

How did I get here?
What have I done?
The river rages on, swollen
with tears.

I can't help you,
I can't help myself ,
I've tried so hard, and failed
so badly.

A hidden vision half a breath away…
quiet, sparkling, crystal water,
effervescent spirit, full of delight.

But I cannot go there
for there are others in the boat
and I cannot leave them to the river.

And the Lord said, "Go, I will be with them."

✻

"The Lord is a refuge for the oppressed,
a stronghold in times of trouble."
PSALM 9:9

✻

"Those who sow in tears will reap
with songs of joy."
PSALM 126:5

THE MICROPHONE

I don't know what I expect Lord, but in my
great vanity
I want to be recognized
I want to be appreciated

In seeking glory for myself
I seem to have lost sight of the glory of God.

When I feel so insignificant I ask,
"Won't someone notice me and
complement me?
Won't someone need me and
appreciate me?"

As if this would make me more important.

Why do I feel this need to be measured and judged and
approved of by man?
Why can't I be content to simply, quietly, humbly be,
and in this way open
myself to be used by God?

— Marjorie Meachum Fedor —

When we think about it, do we praise the microphone
for its voice, its wisdom, its intelligence?
All it really does is stay plugged in and open so
as to amplify the voice of the speaker. But we do
not count the microphone as insignificant, for it
enables the speaker to be heard.

When the "individual" plugs into the source of real
power and becomes an open channel through which
God may speak, that individual is not insignificant in
the eyes of God.
And it is the scrutiny of those eyes that matter.
The love of God is all that matters.

Lord, remove from me the desire for personal
recognition and adoration and help me to want only to
serve You. And help me, Lord, to recognize that I must
prepare myself with knowledge about You if I am to
serve You.

*"The unfolding of your words gives light; it gives
understanding to the simple."*
PSALM 119:130

THE STORY OF TWO SPARKLING BITS

Two sparkling bits in the universe began considering their needs.

They agreed on their need for love and recognition.

One became fearful of not receiving this, and began looking in, to himself—and he reached out only to take for himself. The more he looked in, the smaller he became—the more he reached out to take, the faster everything moved, and the darker it became. And everything he touched became the same.

The other was less fearful, and turned his eyes outward, and upward.
And the more he saw the brighter it became. And he spread himself out, and there was warmth and light. And he never really saw himself—he just reached out and touched, and gave, and was happy.

One became a sun,

the other a black hole.

"The Lord is with you when you are with Him.
If you seek Him He will
be found by you, but if you forsake Him,
He will forsake you."
2 CHRONICLES 15: 2

"It is more blessed to give than to receive."
ACTS 20:35

— Marjorie Meachum Fedor —

Winter Tree

Bereft of color and of leaves
I stand bleak and barren.
Winter came without my knowing,
empty branches, muffled pulse, lost dreams.

Surely glistening jewels of spring will
dance all 'round again and wake
this numb and silent heart.

Surely warmth will come, and with it
bright green leaves, and fruit for harvest.

Oh, spring…be not long in coming.

✳

*"To everything there is a season, a time for every purpose
under heaven."*
ECCLESIASTES 3:1 (NKJV)

EYE OF THE NEEDLE

The trouble is I sometimes see myself in
these puffed-up terms
Really something special…sort of Your
"gift to the world."

But at the same time I see the
other part of me,
And wonder which is real and which is mask.

Help me to see that I am but the eye
of the needle.
You are the thread and the hand that
guides each stitch.

I do not fail.
I only fail to be in your service.

I do not succeed.
I succeed in allowing myself to be
guided by You.

The finish is hidden in a future only
You can see.
I can only wonder at the final results.
Perhaps a glorious tapestry
With brilliant hues and threads of gold and silver
That will inspire awe for Your majesty and power.

Or perhaps, a simple, brightly-colored soft, quilt
That will bring such warmth and love and joy to all
who touch it
That they will feel Your presence and
know Your love.

Yes…that would be nice.

✹

*"Humble yourselves, therefore,
under God's mighty hand,
that He may lift you up in due time."*
1 PETER 5:6

Rainbow Slide

There is quiet
waiting
patience
slip away
too cool, too sure
A mask of calm, the drone of words
to hide the fear and confusion..

Wake up
come back
touch
feel the warmth.

Risk
that wondrous balance point
pivoting
choosing
taste the honey
drink the nectar

— Marjorie Meachum Fedor —

splash in icy waters
rest on sun-baked rocks
slide on rainbow colors
in the quest for gold.

Sometimes Peace
Sometimes Pleasure
Sometimes Pain
Savor all life has to give.

✳

"The Lord will fulfill His purpose for me;
Your love, O Lord endures forever."
PSALM 138:8

— Marjorie Meachum Fedor —

MOVE TOWARD THE MOUNTAIN

I hover above the moment wrapped in a cloak of
silence, reluctant to engage.

The past is muddied with hurt and pain and regret. The
future is obscure in the clouds of unpredictability and
potential disappointment. Just to consider it takes more
energy than I can muster.

I move toward the mountain—no one sees me there—
I can settle in and be.

❋

> *"I will lift up my eyes to the hills—*
> *from whence comes my help?*
> *My help comes from the Lord who*
> *made heaven and earth.*
> PSALM 121: 1,2 (NKJV)

THE MOUNTAIN

I hide myself with God in the quiet of the mountain. His creation speaks to me in chirp and drone and song, carried by the gentle breeze that whispers through the leaves. I answer with heartbeat and breath, and the sound of my steps on the path.

The air is clean and cool and fragrant...now and then a sweet, heady, woodsy aroma surrounds me as I walk. Water from a secret spring high in the mountain ripples down through rocks and fallen leaves, to meet with other streams no doubt, going to who knows where.

Each plant and tree adds a shape and green of its own. There are flowers...trillium, violets and wild strawberries are tucked away, seen only by those who care to look. Laurel, daisies and blackberry bushes are open with their show. But mostly there is green...rich and real and close.

The sky is light gray, with an occasional startling

reward of a yellow sun-shaft that shines on a patch of trees and forest floor. Tattletale thunder announces a gathering storm in the distance. Likely it will pass by on some other mountain.

The peace and strength and love of God quietly encompass me. I am suspended in time, without past or future. For now there is this present time, and it is everything.

✳

"You will go out in joy
and be led forth in peace;
the mountains and hills will burst
into song before you,
and all the trees of the field
will clap their hands."
ISAIAH 55:12

RAINBOWS

Thank God for rainbows, because sometimes the storms are so dark and frightening.

When things are peaceful and perfect I am in a beautiful field of grass and flowers, dotted with sturdy trees. A pond of clear water lies at the bottom of the hill reflecting the enormous blue sky. There are birds in the trees, and a drone of invisible creatures. The sun is warm and I never want to move from this spot.

I would stay here forever, but the breeze that has cooled my face now makes the grass bow down, and the white clouds begin racing across the sky. I feel anticipation, an excitement in the change—the unknown, but it grows so dark. The friendly trees become shadows. The pond, and sky, and the flowers are gray. I am not sure if I am cold because of the rain or because of the fear that is beginning to chill my heart.

Why? Why? Why has this happened? Everything was so perfect.

I know I have to leave this place, but things are so different now, and I don't know which way to go. I remember a path I once saw, but never thought of following. I move toward it. I don't know where it leads, but somehow it feels right.

At first I hardly notice that it is not as dark as it was. Then, there are rays of light at the top of the hill. By the time I get there the sun has broken through the clouds. I look down and the beauty takes my breath away. There is a valley below with fruit trees and flowers cut by a ribbon of blue water. And there are homes shining white in the sun.

Well beyond the valley there is a glimpse of a distant sea, and for a moment I wonder about the sea. But that thought is lost for now as I make my way toward the sounds of laughter and the smell of blossoms.

As my shoes crunch the gravel on the path I remember for an instant the thunder of the storm. I smile as I realize, if it were not for the storm I would not have come to this place.

No matter how severe the storm may be God is there with you.

In Genesis 9:16, God tells Noah,

"Whenever the rainbow appears in the clouds, I will see it and remember the everlasting covenant between God and all living creatures of every kind on the earth."

This is not only a promise for the world, but for "me" as well. In the worst of times God remembers me—He is present with me—He will see me through.

Watch for the rainbows!

CALM

(Christ Always Loves Me)

*"Always be full of joy in the Lord. I say it again—
rejoice! Let everyone see that you are considerate in all
you do. Remember, the Lord is coming soon.*

*Don't worry about anything; instead, pray about
everything. Tell God what you need, and thank him for
all he has done. If you do this, you will experience God's
peace, which is far more wonderful than the human
mind can understand. His peace will guard your hearts
and minds as you live in Christ Jesus.*

*And now, dear brothers and sisters, let me say one more
thing as I close this letter. Fix your thoughts on what is
true and honorable and right. Think about things that
are pure and lovely and admirable. Think about things
that are excellent and worthy of praise. Keep putting
into practice all you learned from me and heard from me
and saw me doing, and the God of peace will
be with you."*

PHILIPPIANS 4:4-9 (NLT)

Printed in the United States
3049

9 781931 232388